NEWLYWEDS'
GUIDE
TO SEX
ON
THE FIRST
NIGHT

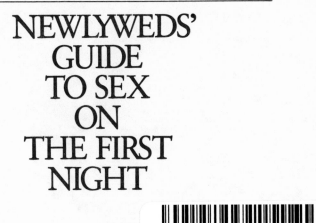

NEWLYWEDS' GUIDE TO SEX ON THE FIRST NIGHT

by Richard Smith

WORKMAN PUBLISHING
NEW YORK

Library of Congress Cataloging in Publication Data
Smith, Richard.
Newlyweds' guide to sex on the first night.
1. Sex—Anecdotes, facetiae, satire, etc.   2. Honey-
moon—Anecdotes, facetiae, satire, etc.   I. Title.
PN6231.S54S576   1985   818'.5402   84-40318
ISBN 0-89480-773-0

Book and cover design: Paul Hanson

Workman Publishing Company, Inc.
1 West 39 Street
New York, New York 10018
Manufactured in the United States of America
First printing April 1985
10 9 8 7 6 5 4 3 2 1

Dedication

To all the bachelors
who have gone before me
and to all the brides
who have come after me.

CONTENTS

Part One
PRENUPTIAL ADVICE

Part Two
PLANNING YOUR HONEYMOON

Part Five

SURVIVING THE WEDDING NIGHT JITTERS

Part Six

HONEYMOON MEMORIES

INTRODUCTION

*"Sex may lead to marriage, but marriage doesn't
always lead to sex."*

What happens when two people, at last joined in
matrimony, realize they can make love all they
want but don't quite know how?

Although the wedding is over, the honeymoon is
just beginning—after months, perhaps years of denial,
they can now enjoy sex legally, their passion restricted
only by the groom's athletic prowess, the bride's stamina, and the tensile strength of the marriage bed.

Unfortunately, however, many newlyweds, because
of limited sexual experience or, worse, unlimited sexual
experience but with incompetent partners, often find
the first night of their honeymoon filled with disaster.
The bride wants to feel sensual but cannot—she's busy
writing thank-you notes. The groom, finally alone with
his bride, may feel anxious and lock himself in the
bathroom, refusing to emerge unless she promises not to
stare. In many cases, fears and misconceptions may ruin
all efforts at achieving sexual pleasure. The bride may
feel cheated upon discovering that even perfect foreplay
does not erase crow's feet. The groom, recalling his
grandmother's advice, may insist on the aphrodisiac
powers of goat cheese, then wonder why his bride
demands an annulment. And both, in their naïveté, may
find their first attempts at coitus severely hindered by an
unfortunate choice of position, unaware that the missionary, although reliable, makes little provision for
both partners on top.

One answer, it would seem, is to begin the honeymoon and hope for the best or for advice from a kindly
bellhop. Another solution might be a sex manual, one of
the many promising "ultimate pleasure." These books,
however, often cause more problems than they solve. To
begin with, they are technically complicated—a mechanically inclined couple may find, after carefully following the first chapter, that rather than achieving sexual bliss, they've somehow assembled a porch swing.

Worse, these manuals, usually written by a sex therapist, offer scientific terminology that renders much of their contents puzzling. It is, indeed, the precocious couple who, with little or no experience, will readily grasp the meaning of subtleties like "giggling," "ecstasy," "support garment," "lox," "user-friendly," "love cries," "wet spot," and "suggested readings."

Therefore the *Newlyweds' Guide to Sex on the First Night*—a "starter" sex manual that eliminates first-night trauma—gives uncompromisingly honest answers to questions most agonized over by honeymooners: "When should we unpack?" "Who undresses first?" "Are bedsores contagious?" "Can we do it again in the morning?" "Are boxer shorts sufficient grounds for annulment?" and many more.

To be sure, experience is the best teacher except in sex, where a teacher is the best teacher. Therefore, until you're both completely comfortable with each other, allow your own common sense, the *Newlyweds' Guide,* and an out-of-control pulse rate to be your guide.

THE HONEYMOON RITUALS

B ecause there's so much to do and, in many cases, so little time, newlyweds may wish to pay particular attention to the "Honeymoon Ritual" pages throughout the book, which contain suggested time allotments for those sexual activities that are indispensable for a perfect wedding night. Figures are, of course, variable since vital factors such as length of honeymoon, size of each partner's erogenous zones and how many he or she has (a big partner may have as many as 20, a little partner only 2.4) must be taken into account. Some examples:

Stimulating Partner to Ecstasy	Time Required*
(Goes chiefly according to body size)	

If he's: Average	.21 minutes, 4 seconds
A hunk	.47 minutes
A midget	.2 minutes
A space cadet	.200 minutes

If she's: Petite	.6 minutes
Very petite (difficult to find among the covers)	.22 minutes
Junior Miss	.34 minutes, 7 seconds
Full-size	.40 minutes
Amazonian	.125 minutes

*Time and motion studies by computer imaging.

Recovering from Carrying Bride over the Threshold	Time Required
Bride	2 minutes
Groom	70 minutes
If bride didn't want to cross threshold.....	216 minutes

Surviving a Rich, Fulfilling Climax	Time Required
Typical time span before you are able to:	
Loosen grip on purse	2 minutes
Stop twitching	3 minutes
Un-grit teeth	5 minutes
Utter a coherent sentence..........	9 minutes
Demand another, without frightening partner	30 minutes
(*Note:* If partner exhibits symptoms of orgasmic burnouts, wait at least one hour.)	
Vote intelligently...............	56 minutes

THE NATIONAL HONEYMOON SURVEY

It is not unusual for newlyweds to wonder—How do we compare with other honeymoon couples? The following statistics were compiled during a survey of 17,362 average American honeymooners. But a word of caution—strict comparisons are not only foolish, they could be severely detrimental to one's health and well-being if taken too seriously. Therefore, we have omitted figures of an anxiety-inducing nature, such as how often the typical bride and groom do it (76 times per week, slightly more during the busy season) and the number of orgasms sustained each time by the satisfied bride (16).

Two Primary Sources of Nourishment for Couples Reluctant to Leave Their Room:

1. Room service
2. Photosynthesis

Four Most Popular Sex Manuals:

1. *The Joy of Sex*
2. *The Kama Sutra*
3. *The Sears Catalog*
4. *Winning Through Intimidation*

Eight Most-Followed Self-Improvement Articles:

1. *Mademoiselle:* "How to Lose Weight"
2. *Glamour:* "When to Lose Weight"
3. *Redbook:* "Should You Lose Weight?"
4. *Ladies' Home Journal:* "Why Lose Weight?"
5. *National Geographic:* "Where to Lose Weight"
6. *Cosmopolitan:* "How Much Do You Weigh?"
7. *Psychology Today:* "How Much Should You Weigh?"
8. *Gourmet:* "How to Gain Weight"

Most Difficult Decision Faced by Newlyweds:

When to leave the guests

Least Difficult Decision Faced by Newlyweds:

When to take the guests along

Carrying the Bride over the Threshold—Odds of Dropping Her if She's Partial To:

Health food: 1 in 90
Nouvelle Cuisine: 1 in 75
Italian (*southern*): 1 in 10
Italian (*northern*): 1 in 40
French (*but hates desserts*): 1 in 25
French (*can't resist desserts*): 1 in 3
Chinese: 1 in 15
Mexican: 1 in 2

Average Time Elapsed Between Checking into Honeymoon Resort and Consummation of Marriage:

Most typical: 57 minutes
Least typical: 1 minute, 44 seconds

Three People Most Likely to Violate Your "Do Not Disturb" Sign:

1. Misinformed house detective
2. Avon lady
3. Jehovah's Witness

Groom's Two Greatest Anxieties:

1. She'll wear me out
2. How much to tip the bellhop

Bride's One Greatest Anxiety:

1. What to do with four toaster ovens

Time Required for Bride to Arouse the Groom:

Left-handed: 6 minutes
Right-handed: 2 minutes, 8 seconds

The Male Erection:

Average length: 6.4 inches
Above average length: 40 inches
Average length as first perceived by frightened
bride: 17 feet

Most Popular Sexual Aid:

Love handles

Least Popular Sexual Aid:

The best man

Most Diabolical Sexual Aid:

Overalls

Groom's Favorite Sexual Stimuli:

1. The bride
2. Hunting season

Groom's Least Favorite Sexual Stimulus:

Mice

The First Night—Excuse Least Frequently Used for Not Having Sex:

"We'll wake the children."

The First Day—Excuse Most Frequently Used for Not Having Sex Underwater:

"We'll wake the fish."

The First Time—Attempting Insertion—Average Number of Misses by Groom:

OUTDOORS: In a hammock: 6
Only one end tied to a tree: 55

INDOORS: On cotton sheets: 3
On satin sheets: 17
On a vibrating bed: 109

Oral Sex—Mistake Most Often Made by the Inexperienced:

Trying it under the covers

Oral Sex—Most Aggravating Aspect:

Hair

Oral Sex—Two Most Effective Removal Implements:

1. Coughing
2. A plunger

Average Time Required to Insert Diaphragm:

By bride: 2 minutes (a tad more if she's still being carried
        over the threshold)
By helpful groom: 2 weeks

Average Time Required to Achieve Erection:

Under ideal circumstances: 34 seconds
At a sperm bank: 10 hours

Best Type of Orgasm to Have:

Partner notices

Three Most Energy-Consuming, Post-Coital Activities:

INDOORS: 1. Searching for a contact lens
        2. Flipping the mattress
        3. Avoiding the wet spot

OUTDOORS: Extracting splinters

Most Prevalent Honeymoon Affliction:

Bedsores

Two Chief Sources of Guilt:

1. Too much pleasure
2. Paying for room with a stolen credit card

Part One

PRENUPTIAL ADVICE

The logistics of planning a wedding—preparing the guest list, choosing a caterer, selecting the ring, newspaper announcements, the rehearsal dinner, even how to call the whole thing off—all pale in comparison to more immediate problems, namely: Should you get married? Should you marry for love? For sex? Is it possible to marry for both? And, perhaps most important of all, how far can you go before the ceremony or, for those who disdain tradition, during the ceremony?

In this section, we shed light on those aspects of marriage so often omitted by ordinary "marriage" manuals and almost totally neglected by even the most experienced clergymen.

WHY ARE YOU GETTING MARRIED?

A brief listing to help you confirm what you probably already know.

Mature Reasons	Very Mature Reasons
Ready for commitment (to a partner)	Ready for commitment (to a sanitarium)
Parents no longer need you	Parents no longer want you
Do not wish to be a social outcast	Biological clock ticking
For American citizenship	For money
For love	For love, sex and money
Regular sex with a known person	Irregular sex with a known person
Her dimples	Her chili
His cleft	His apartment
Hate TV dinners	Hate own cooking
Need a victim when testing new recipes	Need a victim
Want her to be the mother of my children	Want her record collection
Need help with the rent	Need help with the mortgage

ARE YOU READY FOR MARRIAGE?

The degree of sexual maturity needed to ensure a happy union is, fortunately, minimal—a smattering of biology and, if possible, at least one premarital erotic experience that did not take place either in a car or a broom closet. The following four-part quiz, prepared by the Board of Regents and designed to rate your sexual profile, will help decide whether you need more experience (see "Last Fling," page 32) or are adequately prepared for your wedding night. (*Note:* Do not cheat or ask your partner for help.)

PART I BASIC EXPERIENCE

Have You Ever Made Love:

1. Underwater?	☐ yes	☐ no
Did you squish?	☐ yes	☐ no
Any bubbles?	☐ yes	☐ no
2. In a van?	☐ yes	☐ no
Did you ruin the suspension?	☐ yes	☐ no
3. On an airplane?	☐ yes	☐ no
In the lavatory?	☐ yes	☐ no
At your seat?	☐ yes	☐ no
Was the meal tray down?	☐ yes	☐ no
4. During an office party?	☐ yes	☐ no
5. During a bail hearing?	☐ yes	☐ no

6. At a party?	☐ yes ☐ no
In the bedroom?	☐ yes ☐ no
In the bathroom?	☐ yes ☐ no
On the hors d'oeuvres?	☐ yes ☐ no

| 7. In a Jacuzzi? | ☐ yes ☐ no |

8. While snorkeling?	☐ yes ☐ no
Did the flippers help?	☐ yes ☐ no
	☐ only a little

| 9. In the rear of a taxi? | ☐ yes ☐ no |
| Were you charged extra? | ☐ yes ☐ no |

10. At a beach?	☐ yes ☐ no
On a blanket?	☐ yes ☐ no
Under a blanket?	☐ yes ☐ no
In a sand castle?	☐ yes ☐ no

11. On an elevator?	☐ yes ☐ no
Self-service?	☐ yes ☐ no
With an operator?	☐ yes ☐ no

| 12. While performing a public service (such as running for mayor or watching a parade)? | ☐ yes ☐ no |

| 13. While taking a blood test? | ☐ yes ☐ no |

14. With the aid of a sex toy?	☐ yes ☐ no
An exercycle?	☐ yes ☐ no
A yo-yo?	☐ yes ☐ no
A kitchen timer?	☐ yes ☐ no
Was partner conscious throughout?	☐ yes ☐ no

Part II Ethical Considerations

Have You Ever Had Sex:

1. For a meal? ☐ yes ☐ no
   - In a restaurant? ☐ yes ☐ no
   - Home-cooked? ☐ yes ☐ no
   - Fast-food? ☐ yes ☐ no

2. For a part in a movie? ☐ yes ☐ no
   - A cameo role? ☐ yes ☐ no
   - The lead? ☐ yes ☐ no

3. For money? ☐ yes ☐ no
   - $49.99 or less? ☐ yes ☐ no
   - $50.00 or more? ☐ yes ☐ no

4. To make it through the night? ☐ yes ☐ no

5. To make it through the week? ☐ yes ☐ no

6. Because:
   - You were too tired to refuse? ☐ yes ☐ no
   - Nothing good on television? ☐ yes ☐ no
   - You couldn't say no? ☐ yes ☐ no
   - You never tried it with a Latvian? ☐ yes ☐ no

7. To burn off calories? ☐ yes ☐ no

8. For pleasure:
   - Yours? ☐ yes ☐ no
   - Your partner's? ☐ yes ☐ no

9. For free driving lessons? ☐ yes ☐ no

10. For a passing grade?	☐ yes ☐ no

11. To avoid a speeding ticket?	☐ yes ☐ no

12. To repay a favor?	☐ yes ☐ no
You borrowed your neighbor's lawnmower?	☐ yes ☐ no
You borrowed your neighbor's spouse?	☐ yes ☐ no

13. For the exercise?	☐ yes ☐ no

14. As a charitable contribution?	☐ yes ☐ no

15. For a ride home?	☐ yes ☐ no

16. For a ride in the Space Shuttle?	☐ yes ☐ no

17. For medical reasons?	☐ yes ☐ no
To relieve tension?	☐ yes ☐ no
To improve circulation?	☐ yes ☐ no
To get rid of the flu?	☐ yes ☐ no

PART III EMOTIONAL STABILITY

Are You Oversexed?

1. Have you ever missed more than three days of work because of sex?	☐ yes ☐ no

2. Would you rather make love than make brownies?	☐ yes ☐ no

3. Have you ever promised to give up sex but reneged after three nights?	☐ yes ☐ no

4. Have you ever had sex in the morning and in the evening?	☐ yes ☐ no
With a different partner?	☐ yes ☐ no

5. Do you envy those able to stop after three hours?	☐yes ☐no
6. Do you tell yourself you can stop at any time but find, after five hours, that you still crave more?	☐yes ☐no
7. Have you ever awakened with a "sexual hangover"?	☐yes ☐no
8. Have you ever had physical problems connected with sex: lumbago, difficulty climbing ladders, facial tics?	☐yes ☐no
9. Do you occasionally experience blackouts (can't remember where you left the car at the shopping mall)?	☐yes ☐no
10. Have you ever felt life would be worse without sex?	☐yes ☐no
11. Have you ever felt death would be better with sex?	☐yes ☐no
12. Do orgasms cause you to blink?	☐yes ☐no
13. Has lovemaking ever caused your windows to fog?	☐yes ☐no

PART IV COMPATIBILITY AND ABILITY TO COMPROMISE

Have You Ever Refused to Make Love Because Of:	
1. Indigestion?	☐yes ☐no
2. Ominous horoscope?	☐yes ☐no

3. Precarious hairdo?	☐yes	☐no
4. Allergies?	☐yes	☐no
5. The bed (someone already using it)?	☐yes	☐no

6. Irrational fear:

We'll wake the neighbors?	☐yes	☐no
We'll injure my bowling hand?	☐yes	☐no
The cat's not spayed?	☐yes	☐no

7. Major conflict?

Superbowl in progress?	☐yes	☐no
To be, or not to be?	☐yes	☐no

8. Rigid standards:

Partner not a citizen?	☐yes	☐no
Partner not a Democrat?	☐yes	☐no
Partner not all there?	☐yes	☐no

9. Reluctance to disturb suntan?	☐yes	☐no
10. Lent?	☐yes	☐no
11. Chanukah?	☐yes	☐no

12. False pretense?

Headache	☐yes	☐no

SCORING

Part I

If you answered yes:

0 to 6 times: You have minimal experience. Either begin practicing immediately or marry someone more learned.

7 to 15 times: Suitably experienced. You'll be able to make a substantial contribution to the marital bed.

16 times or more: Very experienced. Your partner, not to mention one or two neighbors, may seek your guidance.

Part II

If you answered yes:

0 to 10 times: Morals of a monk.

11 to 16 times: Morals of a record producer.

17 times or more: Morals of a casting director.

Part III

If you answered yes:

3 to 5 times: Sane, almost boringly so.

6 to 9 times: Neurotic, but delightfully functional.

10 times or more: A psycho, but you're having fun.

Part IV

If you answered yes:

0 to 3 times: A perfect partner.

4 to 8 times: Be certain you're marrying someone who's easygoing and can cope with feelings of irregularity.

10 times or more: Stay single.

YOUR FUTURE PARTNER
What to Look For

Love, of course, does conquer all. It is wise, however, to bear in mind that a partner with fringe benefits—a better stereo system than yours and a winning lottery ticket—is far easier to love than, say, a religious fanatic with bad teeth. Additional vital, but frequently overlooked assets include:

♥ Sane parents. For ideal in-laws, marry an orphan.

♥ Sensitive fingertips. A reliable indicator of one's ability to dispense perfect, tension-releasing back tickles.

♥ Healthy forearms. Indispensable for professional-strength massages.

♥ Delicious skin. Ideal flavors: amaretto nut, heavenly hash, vanilla and fudge ripple.

♥ Low cholesterol count. For more fun at barbecues.

♥ Knows where to buy wholesale.

♥ An appetite less healthy than yours. This will ensure a good supply of leftovers for those late-night snacks.

♥ Coinciding mood swings.

♥ Good genes. Inspect the parents of your intended. Are there any mental problems? Is there a major loss of muscle tone at only fifty years of age? Is their retirement plan paid up?

♥ The strength of a yak. Only those strong enough to start a power mover.

♥ Compatible signs: A Virgo with a Capricorn? Yes. A Libra with a neon? No.

♥ Do you smoke the same brand of cigarettes?

FURTHER CONSIDERATIONS

A woman should ask herself:

1. Will he be able to keep me warm? The more chest hair he has, the lower your fuel bills. *Note:* Don't despair if his torso is bare. It will blossom as he gets older.

2. Are my thighs larger than his? If so, not only will he borrow your leg warmers, think how you'll look together at the beach.

3. Is he good with his hands? Is he user-friendly? *A no-fail test:* Watch him shape a meatloaf.

4. Can he read a French menu?

A man should ask himself:

1. Can she fix a flat?

2. Can she make a perfect martini? Somebody has to.

3. Will she complain if you take all the covers? If so, she may not be a good sport.

4. Is she a Jezebel?

SHOULD YOU MARRY FOR LOVE?

Certainly love has its advantages—you'll be far less resentful should you get a spouse who happens to snore. Those who marry for sex, on the other hand, find they have little time *to* snore. To help you decide which best suits your needs, we list the following:

Marrying for Love	Marrying for Sex
Sex gets better with time	Sex already better, no need to wait
Three meals a day	Three times a day
Each sexual encounter a deep emotional experience	Each sexual encounter a deep experience
Communication vital	Curiosity vital
Share many common interests	Share only one common interest
Eventually all talk, no action	Eventually all action, no talk
Frequent arguments over money	Frequent arguments over position
Love may fade	Body may fade

Note: It is best to marry for both.

WHEN DO YOU STOP DATING OTHER PEOPLE?

Traditionally, the future bride decides this question according to the size of her engagement ring. The larger the diamond, the sooner she stops seeing other men.

Carats	Stop Dating Others
Ten or more	That second
Seven to nine	That day
Four to six	That week
Two to three	That month
One	Take your time
Anything less	Break the engagement

Note: For the groom it's a gradual tapering off, since he may have to explain his marital plans to as many as eight different women. In some cases, he will have to leave town until the day of the wedding.

THE LAST FLING

Defined as incredible sex* with someone you'd never in a million years bring home to Mom, let alone marry, a last fling is the ideal way to bid farewell to your freedom. For a thirtyish bride, this could mean an eighteen-year-old hunk endowed with the I.Q. of a

Bride- or Groom-to-be	Had Last Fling With
Sherry Leitner, secretary	Juan Tuna, busboy
Horace Wallnutt, pilot, El Al	Bambi Footnik, flight attendant
Mable Downs, art historian	Butch Ryan, construction worker
Max Kudd, chauffeur	Priscilla Fagin, kept woman
Seymour ("Sy") Threads, coat manufacturer	Kelly Kelly, office temporary, actress and "kook"
Eloise Garland, loan officer	Boris Fado, venture capitalist
Wanda Erg, Colonel, United States Army	Ignatius Sweeny, hairstylist for the secret service
Betsy Fronde, student	Vehta Johdpur, exchange student
Ernie Bysshe Shelley, poet	Doretta Karma-Leek, exquisite person
Basil Muffington, food writer, Pravda	Shirley Sony, sushi sculptress
Biff Murchison, truckdriver	Prudence Garbo, highway patrol officer
Muffy Paddington, lost soul	Baba Rama Jones, spiritual advisor
Irving Sturgeon, ex-husband	Julia Shark, ex-wife

badger. For a twentyish groom it might be an older, more experienced woman such as his grandmother's best friend. But how to meet that perfect but temporary someone? In a bar? You could be seen. The Personals? There's no time for interviews. Those without resources might take their cue from the following actual case studies:

*Appearance of UFO's during climax

How They Met	Where They Did It
Argument over whether her water was fresh	On the table, then under the table
In-flight fund-raiser	In the lavatory, between pledges
Handel-Manilow concert	In the loge, during the allegretto
Escorted her to opening of a shopping center	Rear seat, front seat, jump seat, trunk
Over dictation	Showroom and freight elevator
Cocktail party hosted by Chilean embassy	Bathroom and interrogation room
She asked him to dance at Inaugural Ball	Washington, D.C.
Demonstration against imperialism	The Plaza, the Fairmont, the Fontainbleu, the Hyatt Regency
"The Dating Game"	His loft
He asked, "What's this yellow pile?"	Her tatami
Shootout	Shoulder of road
Seance held at Burger King	Under his robe
Alimony proceedings	Judge's chambers

ABOUT THE BIRDS AND THE BEES

How do most newlyweds learn about sex? Some never do. Fortunately for others, there are sex education courses and, as a last resort, word of mouth. Additional erotic information may also be obtained from the following:

Good Sources

✔ The prom queen

✔ Self-instruction (you will need a full-length mirror)

✔ Extension courses (mail order)

✔ Training films (NASA)

✔✔ The walls of pay phones

✔✔ Hands-on experience (make sure you ask, first)

✔✔ Keyholes

✔✔ Banned books

Bad Sources

✗ Driver education courses

✗ Well-intentioned, but repressed, parents

✗ Soap operas

✗ Pakistani movies

✗ Shy clergymen or your family physician

✗ Pop-up sex manuals

UNTIL THE WEDDING— HOW FAR SHOULD YOU GO?

The temptation to "go all the way," perhaps even pet below the waist, will be great, especially if you're fond of each other. Those uncertain of what is proper may wish to observe the following guidelines:

Activity	Yes	No
Kissing:		
French *(teeth open, lips apart)*		✔
British *(teeth clenched, lips apart)*	✔	
German *(everything clenched)*	✔	
American *(mouth ajar—open enough to exchange an M & M)*	✔	
Gently blowing in partner's ear		✔
Gently blowing in own ear	✔	
Dancing *(cheek to cheek)*:		
In a dance hall	✔	
In the shower:		
Unchaperoned		✔
Chaperoned	✔	
Caressing above the waist	✔	

Activity	Yes	No
Caressing below the waist *(only to appendix scar)*	✔	
Caressing way below the waist *(to tops of sweat socks)*		✔
Orgasm due to:		
Fondling		✔
Naughty pictures		✔
Intercourse		✔
Getting into medical school		✔
Passing the bar exam	✔	
Puppy learned new trick	✔	
Carnal knowledge	✔	
Sleeping together:		
Fully clothed		✔
With bundling board	✔	
Arousal:		
Using hands		✔
Over the phone	✔	
Back rubs:		
Regular	✔	
Licentious		✔
Writhing:		
From pleasure		✔
From tickling	✔	

Part Two

PLANNING YOUR HONEYMOON

What kind of honeymoon do you want? Serene? Active? Death-defying? Whichever you choose, it is vital that you select the resort that accommodates your particular needs. Newlyweds who wish simply to relax would do well to avoid either a war zone or a working farm. Couples who, in addition to "never a dull moment," demand fabulous sports facilities, should plan accordingly, bearing in mind that while certain activities actually improve sex, others, because of their energy requirements, may lead to premature exhaustion, as noted on the following page.

FAVORITE PASTIMES

Activity	Complements Lovemaking	Hinders Lovemaking
Skiing	✔	
Skiing *(no lift ticket)*		✔
Roller skating *(in rink)*	✔	
Roller skating *(on beach)*		✔
Candlelight dinner	✔	
Candlelight breakfast		✔
Scavenger hunt *(you the hunter)*	✔	
Scavenger hunt *(you the hunted)*		✔
Tennis		✔
Horseback riding	✔	
Waterskiing *(wearing life jacket)*	✔	
Waterskiing *(no life jacket)*		✔
Golf		✔
Swimming *(Australian crawl)*		✔
Swimming *(breast stroke)*	✔	

TIPS FOR A PERFECT HONEYMOON

Don'ts

✗ Don't cheat.

✗ Don't have it on a school night.

✗ Don't bring parents. It may seem cruel, especially after that caterer's bill, but this, after all, is your night. Promise you'll take them on the next one.

✗ Don't bring a pet.

✗ Don't bring children.

✗ Don't bring wedding gifts, no matter how beautiful. A microwave oven may make your luggage somewhat cumbersome.

Do's

♥ Do take the phone off the hook.

♥ Do get a manageable hairdo. Grooming oneself every five minutes can be distracting during lovemaking. The bride, also, should follow this advice.

♥ Do undress at least one hour before making love. This permits the body, like wine, to breathe, thus ensuring greater efficiency.

♥ Do water your plants before leaving.

♥ Do stifle yawns.

♥ Do bring your diary.

♥ Do bring your dowry.

CHOOSING YOUR HONEYMOON RESORT

Too often newlyweds, seduced by colorful brochures promising exciting entertainment, exotic activities, and even a complimentary cocktail, arrive at their destination only to find themselves utterly disappointed. A reliable travel agent* will help you avoid the following atrocities:

What They Promise	What You Get
Rides in a glass-bottom boat	It navigates back and forth across the swimming pool
A duty-free shop	That sells only seashells and muscatel
Aerobics classes	Upon arrival, you are handed a jump rope
A warm welcome	Heat wave in progress
Exciting entertainment	Revolution in progress
Exotic activities	Bingo tournaments
Unforgettable food	Intestinal distress from yogurt crêpes
Complimentary cocktail	Free ice
Daily air show	Mosquitoes

*Also find out if it's a teaching resort. If so, you'll be constantly interrupted by other couples who, in their search for knowledge, will feel free to enter your room to observe.

WHAT TO BRING ALONG

In addition to a suitable wardrobe, there are several items, often overlooked, that are certain to enhance your wedding night. The most vital are:

1. **Champagne.** For the ultimate bubble bath.

2. **Baby oil.** To prevent chafing.

3. **Wedding gifts of a monetary nature.** (To be placed on the bed and gazed at—an alternate form of arousal.)

4. **A change of underwear.**

You may also wish to consider the following—not so vital, but nice to have along:

Your therapist.

Goggles for those tender moments in the sauna, as well as underwater.

Dramamine, or any motion sickness remedy, should you somehow find yourself caught in the whirlpool bath.

Scuba equipment to better take advantage of your heart-shaped tub.

Life jacket in case you encounter white water in your Jacuzzi.

Crash helmet. Head injuries ranked first among honeymooners doing laps across their heart-shaped pool. It will also prevent concussion during feverish sex, when your head keeps pounding the headboard.

Pliers. The bride will find this necessary if her groom is wearing tamper-proof garters.

Flashlight for after-dark skinny dipping.

Non-skid socks. Satin sheets, though luxurious, provide little in the way of traction.

Beeper, should your parents need you.

REACHING YOUR DESTINATION
If You Travel by Air

Although the United Nations has recently passed a resolution declaring all airline foods to be aphrodisiac (Swiss steak being the exception), impatient newlyweds will find that each carrier has its own rules concerning in-flight lovemaking.

Airline	Prohibits
SWISSAIR	Moans that cause radar blips
LUFTHANSA	Everything
ALITALIA	Nothing, as long as it's performed under a blanket
UNITED	Orgasmic undulations unless seat belt securely fastened
TWA	Oral sex with the meal tray up
AMERICAN	Erectile failure (except during turbulence)
EASTERN	Quickies (except on shuttle flights)
AIR FRANCE	Broken promises
THE SPACE SHUTTLE	Fooling around during an experiment

Note: It is a Class A felony to "handle, fondle or stare at" any organ of reproduction over Nebraskan air space.

REACHING YOUR
DESTINATION
If You Travel by Car

A uto travel presents fewer problems since all but nine states permit any activity between consenting adults as long as the seat belts are fastened. Before starting out, be aware of the following restrictions:

State	Offense	Fine
ALABAMA	Arousal in a convertible	$25.00
	With top down	$200.00
CALIFORNIA	Two people in the driver's seat	$50.00
COLORADO	Ignoring her stop sign	$45.37
IOWA	Reckless writhing	$20.00
ILLINOIS	Failure to signal when changing position	$35.00
MICHIGAN	Failure to follow partner's directions	$70.00
OHIO	Failure to stop during climax	$55.00*
PENNSYLVANIA	Blowing horn in an erogenous zone	$60.00
VERMONT	Improper action on curves	$25.00

*2nd violation: $65.00
 3rd violation: $75.00
 4th violation: Suspension of marriage license

THE PERFECT HONEYMOON SUITE

Discriminating honeymooners, tired from a long and possibly arduous trip, will appreciate a well-appointed room. Certainly there will be the inevitable amenities—fragrant soap, fluffy towels and, if the accommodations are truly luxurious, a free sewing kit. To make your wedding night genuinely memorable, however, we feel your room should also have:

1. **Mirrors on the ceiling.** This will enable you to monitor your partner's vital signs—panting, groaning and spasms—all symptoms indicating either a coital position forbidden by the Dutch Chiropractic Institute or the consumption of too many miniature stuffed cabbages. If there are no mirrors, the bride's makeup mirror, affixed to the ceiling with chewing gum (Juicy Fruit works best), should serve as an adequate reflective device.

2. **Rear view mirrors on the bed.** (In case you have to back up.)

3. **A revolving bed.** Certain to enhance lovemaking unless you forget to apply the brakes.* Also, a contraption of this sort will facilitate matters should your partner, during moments of extreme bliss, wish to face Mecca.

4. **A fitness machine.** A light warm-up that includes stretching before making love will prevent those pestiferous leg cramps that so often cause a partner to leap out of bed and begin jumping up and down.

5. **A Gideon Bible.** For spiritual guidance should you forget your King James.

Record: June 8,1981, Tanya's Motel and Beauty Parlor, Altoona, Pa. Overcome by centrifugal force, honeymooning couple spins out of control on a revolving bed. They wake up in Ohio.

6. **A parrot chair suspended from the ceiling.** Although chiropractors insist that sex in this device may lead to injury (especially if the chain breaks), we feel it to be a logical alternative to more mundane locations, such as your bed or the night table.

7. **Bathtub decals.** Not merely a safety precaution. It provides something to stare at when washing your feet.

8. **Music.** It is best not to trust the local radio stations, especially if you honeymoon in Borneo. Instead, we suggest your own favorite cassettes to ensure an appropriately romantic atmosphere. If you're at a loss, consider Frank Sinatra, Nat King Cole or, for the high-spirited, Xavier Cugat.

9. **Stationery.** If things get out of hand, you may have to slide distress notes under the door.

10. **Plants.** To provide additional oxygen in case the hotel's supply is inadequate.

11. **Stretcher.** A precaution should either partner begin to ferment.

FINANCIAL RESPONSIBILITIES

Bride Pays For:

✔ Whimsical underwear

✔ Baby sitter, or nurse for parents

✔ Sexually-related damage to contents of hotel room (ripped sheets, cracked headboard, etc.)

✔ Boarding her cat

✔ Visine

✔ Emergency calls to her hairstylist

✔ Any zany device such as velcro handcuffs

✔ Wedding night Polaroids

✔ Album to keep them in

✔ Wedding gift to groom (baby photo of herself)

✔ Picnic basket filled with supplementary but healthful nourishment: 1 bottle red wine, 2 eggs scrambled, 1 whole wheat bagel and 1 pint pea soup

✔ Appropriate firearm if a shotgun wedding

Groom Pays For:

✔ Ladder (if they're eloping)

✔ Speeding tickets (if he can't wait to reach the hotel)

✔ Bribes and bail

✔ Meals

✔ Cleaning solution to remove "Just Married" graffiti from car

✔ Medical expenses incurred while satisfying bride in unusual locations (lotion for poison ivy, Band-Aids if gored by a bull, solvent to remove grass stains)

✔ Wedding gift to bride (dress shields)

✔ Post-honeymoon blood test (to determine if there's any left)

✔ His mistakes:
　　Her lawyer
　　Her alimony

A WORD ABOUT GRATUITIES—
Tipping Is Standard

For exhibitionistic couples who enjoy being watched during lovemaking, the typical honeymoon resort is likely to abound with willing viewers. Unfortunately, audience participation is seldom included in the honeymoon package; rather, this is considered an extra service for which spectators are usually tipped as follows:*

Maid	.50¢
If she's horrified	.60¢
Bellman	.75¢
Bell captain	$1.00
If he participates	$1.25
Concierge	$2.00
Ski instructor	$1.50
On the slopes	$3.00
Golf pro	10¢
Maître d':	
In the dining room	.50¢
In the bedroom	.80¢
Master of ceremonies	$1.00
With witty comments	$1.25
Night watchman	$3.00

*Applause is extra.

Part Three

THE BLUSHING BRIDE

E ven if you don't blush, even if you're more experienced than he is, be gentle, especially if you find yourself having to assume the role of mentor. New husbands are exquisitely vulnerable—it is not unusual for the modern bride to find herself devoting the first hour of the wedding night to coaxing her partner out of the bathroom or, in extreme cases, asking the fire department to break down the door. Note the following telltale signs of male stress:

- Memory problems. Lovingly sipping champagne from a slipper, but while you're still wearing it.
- Disorientation. Shaving very carefully, but using the handle of the razor.
- Nervous eating. Calling room service and ordering eight club sandwiches. (Another indisputable sign—consuming 6,000 cocktail nuts within a five-minute period.)
- Cowardice. Hiding under the bed or behind the maid.
- Covert procrastination. A two-week shower.
- Inappropriate facial affliction (breaking out in a diaper rash).
- Flossing between his toes.

It is your responsibility to calm and reassure him ("We don't have to do it now" is a far more comforting phrase than "Be quiet and lie down"). Also, under no circumstances:

• Bring up the fact that, with the right man, your typical orgasm could easily power Mexico well into the next century.

QUESTIONS RESOLVED BY MARRIAGE

It is perfectly natural to have anxiety—those post-marital doubts and pre-consummation jitters that may, at the last minute, induce you to bolt from the room and flee to Bolivia. Therefore it may be of some consolation to know that marriage, if nothing else, will ease the following classic fears:

1. Will he call me again?

2. Will I hate myself in the morning?

3. Should I invite him up?

4. Will he still respect me?

5. Should I let him stay over?

6. How far should I let him go?

7. Will I be an old maid?

8. Who takes out the garbage?

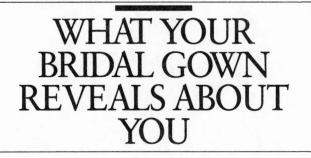

WHAT YOUR BRIDAL GOWN REVEALS ABOUT YOU

The enlightened bride is no fashion slave. In choosing her wedding attire she acknowledges tradition, but first and foremost she selects what's right for her. Guided by good taste, she shuns the garish—paisley and, unless she's a crossing guard, shocking pink. Certainly, despite her virginity (or lack of it), white may be her preference but there are other options:

Color	Meaning
White	Joy, purity, innocence; also assures high visibility in photographs
Red	Joy, purity, innocence; also had lots of fun
Black	Afraid of gravy stains; may also be in mourning over loss of freedom
Green	Totally inexperienced or totally experienced, but Irish
Plaid	Not all that sure she wants to get married, but invitations already sent out
Mauve	Interior decorating a specialty
Yellow	Afraid to get married

"I HAVE SOMETHING TO TELL YOU"

Should you tell him everything? Sharing your most intimate secrets may be what marriage is all about. But it may not be wise to confide in him totally right now. You may want to wait until the honeymoon is over, and everything is paid for, to tell him you've fibbed about your age or that the real you has had a few minor alterations. To help you decide whether complete honesty is, indeed, the best policy, we offer the following suggestions:

Tell Him	Don't Tell Him
Brow lift	Face lift
Forehead lift	Forehead waxed
Herbal wrap	Suction lipectomy
Dermabrasion	Chemical peel
Breast reduction	Breast enlargement
Ears pinned	Tummy tuck (unless it comes undone)
Buttocks lowered (you were too firm)	Buttocks lifted (symbolic defiance of gravity)
Electrolysis (to remove lip hair)	Electrolysis (to remove goatee)
Teeth capped	Nose job
You're not a natural blond	Sex change operation (unless it's not quite finished)

SHOULD YOU BE A VIRGIN?

Most men appreciate a woman with experience, unless it took place on the flight deck of a carrier. On the other hand, if he's not the securest of men, he may feel threatened that you're already a woman of the world. If you decide to be a virgin, be sure you can answer yes to the following questions:

1. Can you blush?

2. Can you act?

3. Could he stand the shock?

4. Can you fake ignorance?

5. Can you fake awe?

6. Can you control yourself? The temptation, during sex, to correct his mistakes ("You're starting without me") will be great.

WHAT IF HE'S A VIRGIN?

For the groom who suddenly discovers that marriage also means "going all the way," the wedding night, especially one that includes sex, can be traumatic. As his understanding bride, it is your role to deflower him as gently as possible; with enough finesse, he may not even realize what's happening until it's too late.

Do	Do Not
1. Be gentle. No sudden moves that may cause him to bolt from the room and fall off the terrace.	1. Introduce advanced technology (latex pantyhose and other enticers) prematurely. Wait until he's comfortable.
2. Explain it won't hurt. But stop immediately if the novocaine begins to wear off.	2. Pressure him to perform. Tugging or tapping it with a seeded roll will only cause anxiety.
3. Allow him questions, no matter how silly. "Is this where it goes?" is common among divinity students.	3. Be too creative the first time. Avoid the temptation to demonstrate your mastery of the Kama Sutra.
4. Show by example. Make friends with the couple next door.	4. Give him a time limit. The sight of you setting a kitchen timer is sure to induce impotence.
5. Let things get out of hand.	5. Doze off in the middle.

THE SEDUCTION

Honeymooners agree that it is much easier to laugh with your clothes off. But should you undress him? For most brides, this can be the beginning of a wondrous, deliciously intimate honeymoon—unless, of course, he's skittish. For your own information we list a few of the more difficult items of apparel to remove, even with dexterous fingers.

Item	Removal Time
Walking shorts	3 minutes
Over his head	2 hours, 14 minutes
Cuff links:	
From long-sleeved shirts	30 seconds
From short-sleeved shirt	30 minutes
Golf bag	19 seconds
Over-the calf socks:	
Pulling down	10 seconds
Pulling up	50 minutes
Undoing belt buckle:	
He helps	8 seconds
No help	15 minutes
Boxer shorts	46 seconds
Briefs	1 minute
Bikini briefs	20 minutes
Tattoo	40 minutes

HIS RECOVERY TIME

M inimal allowable time between orgasms for the average American male.

Occupation	Time Required
Attorney:	
Corporate	43 minutes
Tax	88 minutes
Divorce	200 minutes
Hair Stylist	61 minutes
Doctor:	
Heart specialist	432 minutes
Surgeon (brain)	350 minutes
Surgeon (knee)	20 minutes
Fashion designer	2 minutes
Insurance executive:	
Life	40 minutes
Auto	10 minutes
Investment banker:	
Specialty United States	31 minutes
Specialty South America	260 minutes
Professional athlete:	
Major League	68 minutes
Minor League	59 minutes
Psychiatrist	50 minutes

THE MALE ERECTION*

Until the publication of new research by the League of Nations, innocent brides assumed the stork brought it. Modern science's explanation for this phenomenon, however, is simply that it "gets bigger than it is," when aroused by:

1. You
2. Coaxing
3. A perfect tennis serve
4. An inside stock tip
5. Briquettes that light the first time
6. Memories

But is size really important? Not if it's long enough, suggest most experts—although there are certain men who may feel inferior, due, perhaps, to an organ that during erection resembles a Crayola in heat. For more information, see facing page.

CIRCUMCISION:
Should He Get One?

Advantages	Disadvantages
The perfect gift	May hurt
Makes it more streamlined	Aesthetically unsound
Makes it weigh less	Surgically irreversible
Cooler in summer	Little protection against frostbite
Simple office procedure	Not covered by Workman's Compensation
Very trendy	Doesn't go with everything

TABLE OF LINEAR MEASUREMENT

| HEIGHT OF GROOM | LENGTH IN INCHES | | | |
| | First Night of Honeymoon | | Last Night of Honeymoon | |
	AT REST	ERECT	AT REST	ERECT
5'6"	2.3	4.4[1]	.8	.9
5'7"	2.5	4.7	1.1	1.0
5'8"	2.7[2]	4.9	1.3[3]	1.1
5'9"	2.8	5.1	1.36	1.39
5'10"	2.9	5.4	1.41	1.5
5'11"	3	5.7[4]	1.5	1.7[6]
6'	3.2	6.0	1.6	1.8
6'1"	3.3	6.3[5]	1.8	1.9
6'2"	3.4	6.7[7]	1.9	2.0
6'3"	3.5	6.9	2.0	2.1[8]
6'4"	3.7	7.1[9]	2.2	2.3[10]
6'5" and up	It only becomes wider.[11]			

*Other than sex, it is of no use whatsoever.

[1]Add one inch for Turks in heat.
[2]Subtract one inch for vegetarians and politicians.
[3]Add three inches for member of any tribe inhabiting a rain forest.
[4]Double if a sumo wrestler.
[5]Subtract four inches if caught between closing doors of any uptown subway.
[6]Grounds for annulment in Missouri.
[7]Not applicable after three tequila sunrises.
[8]Cease all sexual activity if it begins to shred.
[9]Caution: may snap off.
[10]Do not offer condolences.
[11]May cause owner some discomfort if bent into a U-shape.

TERMS OF ENDEARMENT

According to tradition, a new bride may exercise the privilege of naming her newest flower—a simple rite in which she takes a swizzle stick and, while *gently* tapping it, utters the phrase, "I dub thee Sir _____."

But what to name it? Reggie? Nicely casual yet strangely formal. Ignatius? Not bad, but possibly demeaning should you lapse into the more familiar "Iggy." "Mordecai?" Too ethnic. The final choice, of course, is yours. You may wish to name it after a favorite uncle or, out of gratitude, a beloved hairdresser ("Troy" is nice). The only taboos are trademarked products—do not use "Ajax," "Comet," or "Top Job." If you are at a loss, feel free to select from the following list of approved names:

Beowulf: Old Norse for "huge, powerful, but the mustache has to go."

Binky: Russian for "Little Twig."

Binkala: Yiddish variation of above.

Bubba: Middle Swahili for "Little Fella."

Caspar: Wyoming dialect for "Loins of Fire."

Delightful Little Cucumber: Origin unknown.

Elmo: from the Dutch meaning "upright, straining towards the sky; in an emergency, will fit into a dike."

Frank: Old High German for "object that fits nicely into a bun, but hold the mustard."

Fyodor: Astrological nomenclature for those born between Libra lowering and Scorpio rising.

Gemini: Only if it has a twin.

John-Thomas: Welsh informal for "Big Boy."

My Little Pickle: English for "My Little Pickle."

Persky: Polish occult meaning "sensitive, vulnerable, but wilts when snapped with a rubber band."

Rex: Gypsy name meaning "bent but not bowed."

Rocco: Sicilian for "eruptive, volcanic, but rather cute when anointed with olive oil."

Salvador: Spanish and South Bronx meaning "firm, constant, overflowing with courage unless frightened by a lunar eclipse."

Slim: Texan for "not fat, goes anywhere without a fuss."

Sparticus: Greek for "hardworking but naughty minnow."

Sweetest Little Sausage: Popular diminutive of "Great Big Sausage."

Thor: From Icelandic *Thorazine,* meaning "undroopable and unstoppable."

MALE BEHAVIOR AFTER ORGASM

Did he have an orgasm? With most men, the signs are obvious—heavy eyelids, lower pulse rate, and a tendency to ignore you. Was it satisfying? Check below:

Behavior	Quality of Orgasm
✔ Pleads for lox	★ ★ ★
✔ Insists he heard sleigh bells	★ ★ ★ ★
✔ Falls into a coma, must be fed intravenously	★ ★ ★ ★ ★ ★ ★ ★ ★ ★
✔ Rolls over and goes to sleep	★
✔ Rolls over and goes to sleep, but tries to take you with him	★ ★
✔ Lights up a cigarette	★ ★ ★
✔ Puts one out	★
✔ Babbles in Swahili	★ ★
✔ Recites, letter perfect, his bar mitzvah speech	★ ★ ★ ★ ★
✔ Showers immediately	✔

Special Quality-of-Orgasm Key

★ Good
★ ★ Above average
★ ★ ★ Excellent
★ ★ ★ ★ Fantastic, worth price of room
★ ★ ★ ★ ★ Possibly the best any human being ever had
★ ★ ★ ★ ★ ★ ★ ★ ★ ★ A Best Bet

COPING WITH BOREDOM

What if he's taking too long to finish? For many women, until they learn yoga, a major problem is what to think about during those interminable minutes when a less-than-spontaneous male may require as many as 4,839 strokes to climax. Because it is inappropriate to lacquer your nails or relax in a chair until he's finished, we suggest any or all of the following ten topics of contemplation:

1. New drapes for the living room.

2. A career change.

3. A position change—from, say, secretary to junior executive, or you on the top and him on the bottom.

4. To whom you still owe thank-you notes.

5. How many credits to go for your MBA.

6. Your stock portfolio.

7. Will the wedding photos turn out?

8. Your new in-laws.

9. What you want out of marriage.

10. Alphabetizing your recipe file.

FRIGIDITY

Nothing seems to be going quite right: At the wedding, despite your pleas, your adenoidal niece sang "Tomorrow"; you're finally married but he still insists on splitting the check; when you threw the bridal bouquet, the caterer caught it. In other words, it's been a long and hectic day, you're in strange surroundings and, to make things worse, he drove there with an expired license. So don't worry if you experience difficulty achieving even a modest climax (.000000002 on the Richter scale). Be comforted to know that wedding night anxiety is perfectly normal, especially when caused by any of the following:

1. In-law trouble (they're in the room).

2. Seasickness (your first experience on a waterbed).

3. Motion sickness (you're table hopping).

4. You're not giving yourself permission.

5. Your new husband looked better with his clothes on.

6. Shriners' convention in the next room.

7. Acrophobia (bed too high).

8. Agoraphobia (bed too vast).

9. Static cling.

Honeymoon Etiquette
YOUR ORGASM— WHO'S RESPONSIBLE?

You are, but only for the first three. Responsibility for additional orgasms may be allotted as follows:

4 to 7: the groom
8 to 11: your therapist
12 to 20: the government
21 and up: back to you

FAKING ORGASM*

Whether it's to preserve his ego or your sanity, or whether the position in which you're making love is causing your leg to fall asleep, a faked climax is perfectly acceptable. Be aware, however, that the time required may exceed that of a natural orgasm, as noted below:

Type of Orgasm Faked	Time Usually Required
Convincing:	
Out-of-body experience . . . . .10 minutes	
Out-of-bed experience . . . . .17 minutes	
(If he's a perfectionist) . . . . .35 minutes	
Unconvincing:	
Out-of-room experience . . . . .96 minutes (Very impressive but seldom works)	
Supplementary:	
Earth moved . . . . .8 minutes	
So did Mars .45 minutes	
Paint peeled . . . . .60 minutes	

*May be habit forming. See your doctor.

THE BRIDE'S RESPONSIBILITIES

Before Sex:

✔ Has the car washed

✔ Explains the meaning of lust (demonstrates, if necessary)

✔ Checks legs for stubble

✔ Leaves seat up

✔ Doesn't peruse the "Help Wanted" section while waiting for groom to overcome performance anxiety

✔ Doesn't call her astrologer

✔ Is considerate: Won't try to excite him by nibbling his earlobe with her wisdom teeth

✔ Waits until after sex to tuck him in

During Sex:

✔ Guides it

✔ Acts impressed

✔ Doesn't insist on the one position certain to throw his back out

✔ Doesn't ask about tax shelters while groom is climaxing

✔ Doesn't tease if groom's flower suddenly wilts

✔ Doesn't laugh if groom misses

After Sex:

✔ Increases volume on television

✔ Consoles groom if first time a disaster

✔ Reaffirms marriage vows if it wasn't

Part Four

THE INEXPERIENCED GROOM

It was the scariest night of my life. I thought she was shy and innocent. Then our honeymoon began and I thought I'd die. Except for catnaps, sleep was out. It was a decathlon without the sneakers. Good thing we brought oxygen.

—Overjoyed Groom

The myth of the innocent bride. Perhaps it's the Jacuzzi, the free hors d'oeuvres, or her first sight of you in nothing but garters and over-the-calf socks. Whatever the reason, the spectacle of feminine passion unleashed can be devastating for the toughest of grooms, be he a professional boxer, or even a tax attorney. In this section, we ease the fears of the new husband by providing insight into what might be termed "male wedding night etiquette."

SHOULD YOU CARRY YOUR BRIDE OVER THE THRESHOLD?

Her Weight *(in pounds)*	Your Course of Action
90 *to* 110	Should be no problem unless you weigh less than she does.
111 *to* 140	Yes, but be certain you're in condition; if necessary, ask her to lighten the load by removing her corsage.
141 *to* 175	Call room service for assistance.
176 *and up*	Simply hold the door open.

If you're still not certain, consider the following:

Pros	Cons
1. Tradition.	*1.* She may not want to cross the threshold.
2. A cardinal act of chivalry.	*2.* Awkward should you drop her.
3. Increases her confidence in your strength.	*3.* You may be too exhausted to do much else.
4. Shows you care.	*4.* She won't be able to wipe her feet.

SHOULD SHE CARRY YOU OVER THE THRESHOLD?

O nly if she earns more money than you do.

THREE ALTERNATIVES
TO CARRYING YOUR BRIDE
OVER THE THRESHOLD

Push her.
Pull her.
Roll her.

UNDRESSING YOUR BRIDE

A nice courtesy if you're not too tired and she's willing to hold still. You'll need extra time to remove some of her more challenging articles of apparel. These include:

1. Her purse.

2. Her chain. It may take up to 30 minutes to open the little catch.

3. A body stocking. Nearly impossible to remove without her full cooperation.

4. The front-loading bra. A diabolical device designed to make men feel mechanically inferior. You'll be particularly ashamed if you assume wrong and work from the back.

5. The bow tie. An extreme accessory favored by women in the fast lane. *Note:* For many men the thought of having to unknot a partner's bow tie before making love is a sure road to impotence.

6. Bikini panties. They inevitably ball up around the ankles and have to be snipped off with scissors. Ditto for bib overalls.

7. Boots. May finally come off with a violent tug, but the force may propel you into the adjoining room. (Galoshes are worse.)

8. A corset. If she wears this gruesome restraining device, be prepared to work through 200 eyelets.

9. Her Walkman.

PERFORMANCE ANXIETY

Considering all he's been through, it would be the unusual groom, indeed, who did not experience some degree of impotence* on his wedding night. Fortunately, there is seldom cause for alarm (unless it's been stung by a bee). With patience and an understanding partner, recovery time can take as little as eight to ten minutes (or eight to ten days if partner is not so understanding). Besides simple stress and strain, there are other reasons for erectile failure. They include:

Minor

- Lack of energy—he's still digesting wedding cake
- Inexperienced bride—she's plucking it
- Insensitive bride—she's snapping it with her garter
- Too much champagne
- Job pressure
- Personal pressure—she's squeezing it too hard

Major

- Intestinal distress—he swallowed the little couple on top of the wedding cake
- Physical discomfort—wedding band on wrong digit
- Vasectomy that morning
- Shock—first time he sees bride without makeup
- Failing school grades
- Impending tax audit

*Defined as "the inability to achieve a visible erection under reasonably erotic circumstances, such as while donating blood or watching the Celtics.

ADDITIONAL WEDDING NIGHT DIFFICULTIES

Climaxing too soon. Known as premature ejaculation,* especially if it takes place during inappropriate moments such as cutting the wedding cake or a marital reconciliation. A groom's orgasm is considered premature if it occurs while:

- On the receiving line
- Inspecting the wedding gifts
- Checking into the honeymoon resort
- Playing a wet 'n' wild polo match

Climaxing not enough. This is known as immature ejaculation and may be caused by either a sleep deficit or trying too hard to love, honor and obey. It is also found among men who never grew up. Their climax is often accompanied by:

- Whining, possibly temper tantrums
- Baby talk
- Demands for milk and cookies

WHAT IS A "MATURE EJACULATION"?
The Five Criteria:

1. It occurs as a direct result of sexual activity.
2. His pupils dilate.
3. It makes him smile.
4. His partner participates (willingly).
5. It occurs without benefit of a Dustbuster.

Not a problem if it's simply beginner's luck.

ORAL COMMUNICATION

What is the meaning of those mysterious, barely intelligible phrases so often uttered in the heat of passion? What is the aroused bride really saying?

What You Hear	What She Means
"I didn't know you could last so long."	(We'll never get to eat.)
"I'll try anything."	(Except that.)
"That feels so good."	(I wish everything else did.)
"This sure beats cooking class."	(But not by much.)
"I'm falling off the bed."	(I'm falling off the bed.)
"You're so virile."	(You're mussing my hair.)
"I can hardly move."	(Could you possibly reach the Mallomars?)
"Let's try that again."	(Maybe this time you'll get it right.)
"Am I the first?"	(To endure this.)
"Don't stop."	(We still have two hours until checkout time.)
"Where'd you learn that?"	(Why'd you learn that?)
"I could lie here forever."	(I'd kill for a pizza.)

HER FIRST ORGASM— HOW LONG SHOULD IT TAKE?

Some brides have much on their mind and may have difficulty "letting go." A career woman struggling up the ladder of success, obsessed with sales figures, balance sheets, and why she doesn't yet have a corner office, will require more time than, say, an attendant at Burger King. A glance below will give you some idea of how to pace yourself. (Table reflects time from first kiss to first climax.)

Career	Average Time
Nurse	1 second
Cheerleader	5 minutes
Feminist (active)	2 hours, 14 minutes
Feminist (lapsed)	1 minute
Anchorwoman:	
Local	14 minutes
National	1 hour
Actress	4 hours, 11 minutes
Model	See Ripley's *Believe It or Not*
Stewardess	20 minutes
With seniority	5 minutes

Note: Some women don't experience their first orgasm until their second husband.

DID SHE REALLY ACHIEVE ORGASM?

H ow to tell abolutely:*

Probably

ALLEGRO ASSAI

AAAAAAAAH

For Certain

LENTO

OOOOOOOOOOH

Only a Little One

PRESTO

EEP-EEP

Faked

LARGO

MMM

*Also reliable indicators: The cadenza from "Caro Nome"; the first ten bars of the Mad Scene from "Lucia di Lammermoor"; a rendering of "Tell Me Lovely Shepherd" by William Boyce (accept no substitutes).

THE GROOM'S RESPONSIBILITIES

Before Sex:

✔ Empties the dishwasher

✔ Leaves seat down

✔ Assumes task of positioning video equipment

✔ Doesn't object if bride turns down TV volume

✔ Is considerate—doesn't help bride remove her contact lenses by shaking her

✔ Shaves (face)

✔ Places chewing tobacco in proper receptacle

During Sex:

✔ Doesn't keep glancing at the sports section

✔ Communicates sexual needs with words instead of flash cards

✔ Doesn't moan off-key

✔ Doesn't treat his bride like a Nautilus machine

After Sex:

✔ Asks, "Was it good for you?"

✔ Helps bride on with her Walkman

✔ Lies in the wet spot

Part Five

SURVIVING THE WEDDING NIGHT JITTERS

What do we do after the bellhop leaves?
—ANXIOUS BUT ENTHUSIASTIC COUPLE

Newlyweds who consider sex an appropriate honeymoon activity should read this section with care, and even permit themselves one—or several—"rehearsal" wedding nights. The ceremony is over, you're both finally alone, perhaps for the first time that day, and the next few decisions will be crucial: Succumb immediately to temptation or check in with your parents? Unpack or merely hang up those garments that might wrinkle?* Begin lovemaking slowly and sensuously or swan dive into the Jacuzzi? The following pages will help you prepare for this first and most important night of your marriage. Although broad in scope, this section cannot possibly cover every contingency, and we suggest dialing 911 should either partner suddenly begin to emit radioactivity.

*Speedy unpacking tip: *1.* Hold luggage upside down.
  2. Open it.
  3. You're unpacked.

THIRTEEN STEPS TO A PERFECT WEDDING NIGHT

The following sequence has been found to be the most productive, although not necessarily the most logical. Those who are either pressed for time or outrageously impatient may choose to begin with orgasm.

1. Arousal

2. Put yourselves on hold and call parents (no need to phone if they're in the next room)

3. Foreplay

4. Unpack

5. Oral sex

6. Rest stop

7. Re-apply lip gloss

8. Intercourse (optional)

9. Dismiss the photographer (mandatory)

10. Orgasm

11. Climax (slightly more final than the above)

12. Inspect each other for bruises

13. Order something nourishing from room service

WHAT TO WEAR

B ecause tradition holds that tonight's apparel should not be too abrupt a departure from your wedding outfit, we offer the following fashion advice:

If Wedding Is	Groom Wears	Bride Wears
ULTRA-FORMAL:	Top hat, cutaway jacket, striped long johns (no cuffs), black garters, black socks	Floor-length negligee, veil, gloves, tiara, white satin bunny slippers
FORMAL:	Homburg, plain boxer shorts (little hearts okay), garters, socks optional	Knee-length negligee or sarong, black garter belt, sheer black hose, see-through boots, decorator riding crop
SEMI-FORMAL:	Dark glasses, boutonniere, day-of-the-week briefs, Walkman, pinky ring	Red garter belt, simple gold chain around waist, beret
INFORMAL:	Hawaiian shirt, cuff links, day-of-the-week athletic supporter, sweat socks	T-shirt, leg warmers, camera
BARGAIN:	Nothing	Nothing

OBSERVING THE PROPRIETIES

In our civilized society, the essentials of courtesy dictate that the occupant of a bathroom must never be rushed. This rule is particularly inviolable on the wedding night when, besides its usual functions, this room becomes nearly sacrosanct, a safety zone where bride or groom, in private, can perform their own preparatory rituals without appearing foolish. But what really happens behind the closed door? To help you understand this new person in your life and to ease your anxiety when you begin to wonder what's taking so long, we offer the following revelations:

What He Says He's Doing	What He's Really Doing
Bathing	Napping
Shaving	Adding a styling gel to his chest hair
Washing his face	Flexing biceps to see how great he looks
Combing his hair	Cursing a receding hairline
Splashing on aftershave	Standing on the sink to see if his legs are too thin
Getting ready for his bride	Sipping NyQuil
Brushing his teeth	Checking his breath by breathing against the wall

Taking a vitamin	Coping with a fashion emergency (can't undo zipper)
Thinking of you	Reading a magazine
Gargling	Eating oysters

What She Says She's Doing	What She's Really Doing
Applying moisturizer	Wondering if her eyes are too far apart; wishing her nostrils were better matched
Removing makeup	Checking teeth for spinach
Showering	Running the water to muffle her sobs
Freshening up	Consulting Mom on modular phone
Brushing her hair	Examining her bust and wishing it were larger or smaller or firmer or higher
Rinsing her face	Inspecting for blemishes
Getting a breath of fresh air	Having second thoughts; trying to climb out of the window
Singing	Cursing her bikini line
Worrying	Worrying

WEDDING NIGHT FRAGRANCE

As a body enhancer, scent takes up where clothing, traditionally disgarded this night, leaves off. These fragrances have been selected not only for their aromatic properties, but also for their special mind-altering qualities. (*Note:* Avoid cheap scents—they tend, during moments of passion, to boil.)

HE WEARS

Brand	Effect on Bride	Effective Range
ARAMIS	Earthshaking; may cause her to relinquish her share of the covers	4 feet
BRUT	Compelling, intriguing, unexplainable; may cause severe loss of appetite	15 feet
CHAPS	Flared nostrils; inability to wait a decent interval between unpacking and foreplay	7 feet
EAU SAVAGE	Turns her body into one, long erogenous zone	10 feet (less under water)
GIVENCHY	Releases sexual protons usually held in reserve for a rainy day	22 feet
MENNEN	Time warp	1 mile
PACO RABANNE	Unbridled lust and loss of inhibitions	12 feet

SHE WEARS

Brand	Effect on Groom	Effective Range
ANAÏS ANAÏS	Utter collapse	6 feet
BAL À VERSAILLES	Devastating; marked increase in desire often resulting in a visit from local authorities	9 feet
CIE	Curious combination of spiritual growth and drooling	11 feet
CHANEL NO. 5	Intense climax; destruction of bed; room a shambles	Two states
JUNGLE GARDINIA	Babbles love words in Arabic	4 feet
GIORGIO	Triples his staying power	Bi-coastal
HALSTON	Highly increased potency; frequent need for bread pudding and tofu	17 feet
OPIUM	Unconditional surrender; torrid passion, possibly causing a heat rash	20 feet
SCOUNDREL	Heart failure	1 foot
SHALIMAR	Difficulty concentrating on stock options	200 feet
SOPHIA	Hopeless abandon; may attempt to disrobe during wedding ceremony	50 feet
TIGRESS	Bleating	8 feet
WHITE SHOULDERS	Spontaneous orgasm	4 feet

THE WARM-UP

Those who thrive on daily exercise will be gratified to learn that a wedding night need not interfere with their workout. The following regimen, though simple, will keep you in shape while preparing you for the most arduous lovemaking.

Exercise	Minutes
Stretching	5

For those particularly acrobatic positions—groom on top, bride locked in bathroom.

| **Jumping Rope** | 10 |

To increase breathing capacity—gives you the edge over your partner in a contest to see who can climax first.

| **Rowing** | 7 |

Strengthens heart, arms and pecs—ensures a favorable outcome in a contest over who climaxes last.

| **Sit-ups** | 12 |

Firms stomach muscles so partner won't be overly horrified when you undress.

| **Push-ups** | 15 |

Builds upper arms, enabling you to remove dead weight, such as an enormous partner who passes out on top of you.

HOW TO BEGIN

E ventually, you'll breeze through the five approved stages of lovemaking:

STAGE I. Initial. Feelings of lust.

STAGE II. Elementary. Undressing, frontal nudity, teensiest shock* if partner less than anatomically perfect.

STAGE III. Intermediate. Indirect stimulation of the erogenous zones due to windchill factor.

STAGE IV. Advanced. Direct stimulation of the erogenous zones through bumping into each other.

STAGE V. Sophisticated. Sex at night *and* first thing in the morning, although your breakfast might be getting cold.

For now, however, we feel it is wisest to begin slowly, with a back-to-basics approach as noted in the following guidelines:

Do	Don't
Kiss the eyelids.	Kiss the eyeballs.
Lick the eyelashes.	Lick them off (unless false).
Blow into each ear gently.	But not at the same time.
Gently nibble each earlobe.	Swallow ornaments (like an earring).
Kiss the tip of the nose.	Chomp on the tip of the nose.
Bite the nape.	Bite the Adam's apple.

*You may experience a similarly horrifying reaction if partner is wearing tasteless underwear. (Sheltered brides have been known to faint when exposed to bikini briefs stating "Home of the Whopper.")

THE HONEYMOON BED

(optimal dimensions: 80 × 60 inches)

Ordinarily, any flat surface except a picnic table will do. But this is a special night and you'll want things to be perfect.

1. Pillows

2. Little mints (not to be moved until after consummation of marriage)

3. Airbag (opens to prevent orgasm-induced head and neck injuries)

4. Neutral corner (inviolable territory where either partner can rest, unmolested, while catching breath or recovering from palpitations)

5. Fun zone (this is where most activity takes place)

6. Bed belt (necessary when making love on a revolving bed)

7. Video camera (for studying mistakes)

8. Coin-activated Magic Motion control

9. Stack of quarters

10. Telephone (to call room service and parents)

11. Supply of Hershey's Kisses (provide twice the emergency energy of a pound of calf's liver)

12. One pound of calf's liver (for the iron deficient)

13. Kitchen timer (to apportion your time)

14. Rosin bag (for better grip)

15. "Just Married" sign

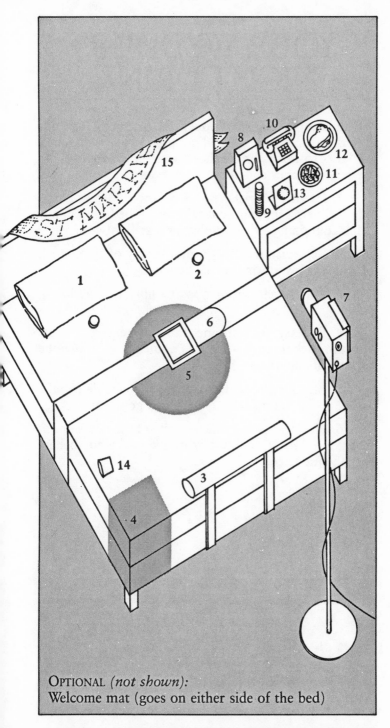

OPTIONAL *(not shown):*
Welcome mat (goes on either side of the bed)

YOUR WEDDING NIGHT DRINK

In addition to their festive qualities, first night libations must be practical, selected not only to help you relax, but also to serve the needs of your body. Ingested in moderation, they should:

1. Provide nourishment. A balanced blend of vitamins, minerals and anti-coagulants can be found in any drink containing either an olive or a stalk of celery.

2. Replenish the body's vital supply of zinc, much of which is lost during sexual activity.

3. Travel well. From glass to lips without losing potency.

4. Be easy to consume and not require aerobic effort to suck through a straw (a notorious example: the frozen banana daiquiri).

5. Blend with the décor. A green crème de menthe frappé will clash mercilessly with orange sheets.

6. Not detract from the sanctity of the occasion. In recent lab tests, a double martini induced giddy behavior in white mice.

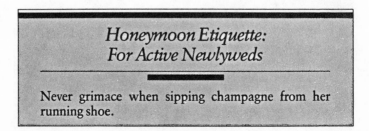

Honeymoon Etiquette: For Active Newlyweds

Never grimace when sipping champagne from her running shoe.

THE PERFECT TOAST

O ffering a toast each time you make love is a favorite wedding night custom. But what are the appropriate drinks? Champagne, of course, goes with everything from saluting the groom's stamina to celebrating the bride's reluctance, after a particularly feeble climax, to press charges. Those, however, unfortunate enough to dislike champagne or who suffer from a bubble allergy may still enjoy the toasting ritual by consulting the following chart:

What to Celebrate	Appropriate Drink
The first time (that night)	Screwdriver, Stinger, Harvey Wallbanger
The tenth time (that night)	Zombie, Brave Bull
A marvelous bondage technique (dental floss and Elmer's Glue)	Mai Tai
Groom's staying power	Singapore Sling
Bride's staying power	Pink Lady, Angel's Kiss
Simultaneous orgasm	Side Car
First time you do it outdoors	Grasshopper
An especial orgasm (bed blew up)	Purple Passion, Planter's Punch

GETTING STARTED
PART I
MENTAL

How to get each other in the mood? In most cases, finally being alone in the privacy of your mountain villa or lakeside suite will provide a sufficiently romantic atmosphere. Of course, if this doesn't work, there's always hypnosis or:

Activity	Minutes to Arousal
Holding hands and staring at the sunset . . . . .35 (Confused newlyweds may try to do this in the morning. This is called a sunrise—allot an extra 30 minutes.)	
Enjoying a long, moonlight stroll: Outdoors . . . . .40 Indoors. 5	
Gazing into each other's eyes: Regular. . . . . .8 If crossed 76	
Insulting each other's parents 5	
Reading poetry together: On the sofa. . . . . .14 Under the covers. 2	
Watching an old movie: *Sands of Iwo Jima*. . . . . .94 *Love Story*. . . . . .28 *Debbie Does Dallas* 3	
Counting the loot. 1	

GETTING STARTED
PART II
PHYSICAL

O nce you are in the mood, follow up with:

Erotic Activity	Minutes to Full Arousal
Moment of silence	1
Showering together:	
Water warm	8
Water cold	40
Washing each other's back:	
Scrub brush	6
Tongue	3
Brushing each other's teeth.	?
(a trendy form of arousal that has not, as yet, been studied)	
Light petting	23
Heavy petting	9
(distinct tingling in extremities)	
Oral sex (just a hint of)	1
Spanking	16
If partner has no imagination	90

FANTASIES

A skillful partner uses fantasy not only to heighten sexual pleasure, but also, during dull or perplexing moments, to help pass the time. Fantasies with a romantic theme should be shared; those more inner-directed are best kept to yourself. Some examples:

Share with Spouse	Don't Share with Spouse
We are making love in a field of clover.	I'm so good in bed that my partner dies from pleasure. I get the insurance.
On an elevator stuck between floors, my partner brings me to climax.	I achieve climax so easily not because of my partner's sexual prowess but because of the seductive Muzak.
We win the lottery and get to throw away the cheap gifts.	We win the lottery and I leave for Brazil.
We're at an orgy, but you're the only partner I want.	I am at an orgy. You're working late.
An old lover returns and tries to seduce me. I refuse.	An old lover returns and tries to seduce me. I refuse because you have better pension benefits.

WHEN DOES PLEASURE BECOME SIN?

Believers are doubtless aware of certain prohibitions placed upon sex. The Koran, for example, forbids orgasm while facing Mecca. Judaism discourages women who maintain a kosher bedroom from engaging in oral sex. To avoid conflicts, be guided by the following chart:

Religious Persuasion	Level of Excitement at Which to Cease Sexual Activity
Hare Krishna	Stuttering while chanting
Moslem	Craving for pork cutlets
Born-again	Religious medal overheating
Buddhist	Enlightenment
Presbyterian	Raised eyebrows
Lutheran	Rapid breathing
Catholic	Heavy breathing
Episcopalian	Heavier breathing
Jewish	Chest pains

AROUSAL
PHASE I

A woman's biggest complaint? That men don't spend enough time on the preliminaries: those little tendernesses—caressing, cuddling, having the ring appraised—that make what happens later even more erotic. But what is reasonable? Thirty seconds of gently blowing in her ear may not be quite enough; three hours, on the other hand, may make her daffy. Here are a few suggestions:

First Intimacies	Time Required
Removing your hat	5 seconds
Deciding which is the optimal side of the bed	1 minute
(*Hint:* the side closest to the bathroom)	
Your first lovers' quarrel	48 minutes
(She also wants that side)	
Taking a long, sensual bath together:	
In a regular tub	15 minutes
In a heart-shaped tub	25 minutes
In a heart-shaped sink	10 seconds
(Economy rooms only)	
Toweling each other dry	5 minutes
Using both sides of towel	3 minutes
Blow-drying each other dry	1 minutes
Back rub for bride	15 minutes
If bride on her back	47 minutes

INTERMISSION

AROUSAL
PHASE II

Not to be commenced until the completion of Phase I.

Permissible Sexual Liberties	Time Required
Warming her up:	
With your arms	9 minutes
With a hot water bottle	2 minutes
(A Best Bet)	
Feeding each other:	
Chocolates	5 minutes
Life Savers	7 minutes
Loin of pork	14 minutes
Petting:	
Above the waist	10 minutes
Below the waist	173 minutes
Around the waist	2 minutes
Covering her with kisses:	
Face:	
High forehead	4 minutes
Low forehead	1 minute
Breasts:	
32aaa	5 seconds
32aa	48 seconds
34b	2 minutes
36b	3 minutes
38c	5 minutes
40dd	60 minutes (happy hour)

FOREPLAY

A t this point, lovemaking becomes more intense and other less erotic thoughts such as the industrialization of Mali seem to fade. Yet, for newlyweds who must budget their time, the temptation to omit the link between innocent petting and final consummation is great. Foreplay, however, need not be neglected if you spend the time as indicated below:

Activity	Time Required
Deciding:	
Who furnishes coin for Magic Motion activator	2 minutes
Where to begin	3 minutes
(Starting at the face and slowly working your way down is considered standard procedure. Starting at the feet and working your way down is not.)	
Coping with typical foreplay "emergencies":	
Partner faints from pleasure	5 minutes
Partner falls out of bed	7 minutes
Partner doesn't notice	52 minutes
Locating erogenous zones:	
Partner helpful, tells you where they are	4 minutes
Partner makes you guess	61 minutes
(*Hint:* If it's quivering, it's probably an erogenous zone)	
Achieving erection:	
For groom	1 minute
For bride	200 minutes

ACTUAL PLAY

This might be considered Level II of Foreplay and spans the fine line between teasing and insertion.

Intercourse	Time Required
Aiming	2 seconds
Missing	51 minutes
Bouncing	12 minutes
Bouncing (head actually makes contact with skylight)	17 minutes
Thrusting (regular)	16 minutes
Thrusting (turbo)	29 minutes
Changing positions	41 seconds
If partner refuses to cooperate	41 minutes
Leaping out of bed (because of a sudden leg cramp)	1 second
Trying to resume where you left off:	
Good memory	1 minute
Bad memory	35 minutes

BIRTH CONTROL METHODS

Options should be weighed carefully, not only with regard to individual preferences, but also with regard to effectiveness. Coitus interruptus, for instance, is safe only so long as one partner, preferably the male, has iron willpower. Coitus uninterruptus is safe so long as one (or more, time permitting) of the following methods is used:

Rhythm Method
SAFE: Duke Ellington

SAFER: Glenn Miller

SAFEST: Cab Calloway

Foam
SAFE: Root beer

SAFER: Guinness Stout

SAFEST: Shaving cream

Withdrawal
SAFE: 10 seconds before climax

SAFER: 10 minutes before climax

SAFEST: 10 days before climax

Luck
SAFE: Four-leaf clover

SAFER: Rabbit's foot

SAFEST: Prayer

Contraceptive Jelly
SAFE: Smucker's blueberry

SAFER: Anne Page's grape (A Best Buy)

SAFEST: Guava

Ungainly Positions
SAFE: Woman on top, man under bed

SAFEST: Both on top

Headache

SAFE: Faked

SAFEST: Real

The Condom:

SAFE: Mosquito netting

SAFER: Tinfoil

SAFEST: Saran Wrap

The Pill

SAFE: M & M's

SAFER: Good 'n' Plenty

SAFEST: Mason Dots

The Diaphragm

SAFE: On him

SAFEST: In her

TROUBLESHOOTING
The three leading causes of first-night catastrophe:

1. Tension—bride's feet are pressed firmly against the ceiling.

2. Phone won't stop ringing—parents know where you're staying.

3. Bellhop won't leave (poor tip—25¢ per bag no longer applies).

PROTECTIVE DEVICES

Putting in Birth Control Device	Time Required
If woman experienced	30 seconds
If woman not experienced	30 minutes
If groom coaching	30 hours

Putting on Birth Control Device	Time Required
With erection	11 seconds
Without erection	11 hours

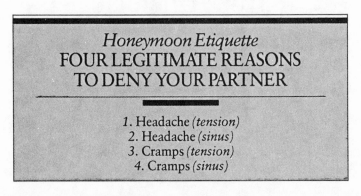

Honeymoon Etiquette
FOUR LEGITIMATE REASONS TO DENY YOUR PARTNER

1. Headache *(tension)*
2. Headache *(sinus)*
3. Cramps *(tension)*
4. Cramps *(sinus)*

CONSUMMATING YOUR MARRIAGE

No matter how intimate the activity—checking into the same hotel room, even attending a couples-only seminar on pottery glazing—your marriage is not officially consummated until you've had intercourse with each other. Those reluctant to indulge may not be aware that:

✔ It's cosmetically beneficial. (Gives skin a youthful glow—up to 75 watts—and firms facial muscles.)

✔ It's inexpensive (never an admission charge).

✔ It can be enjoyed anywhere (except on a chair lift).*

✔ It works the entire body (except on a chair lift).

✔ It's quiet (save for those who heed the call of the wild and emit high-frequency moans).

✔ Educational requirements are minimal (high-school diploma required in Palm Beach).

✔ It's the perfect way to pass on one's religious beliefs.

✔ It has no side effects.

✔ As a form of recreation, it's better than most live shows.

*Or while wearing snowshoes.

THE FIRST TIME

D espite several theories to the contrary, consummation cannot occur without insertion. But how long will this take? A question best answered by stating that aim is everything, especially for those lacking experience or for those with plenty of experience who somehow find themselves on a heaving waterbed.

Insertion	Time Required
Under normal conditions . . . . .15 seconds	
If groom nervous. . . . . .15 minutes	
If bride clenching teeth . . . . .80 minutes	
If bride guiding it . . . . .48 seconds	
If bride retreating . . . . .56 minutes	
Possible delays:	
No erection. . . . . .74 minutes	
Demi-erection .36 minutes	
Myopic groom . . . . .8 minutes	
Lunch . . . . .60 minutes	
Wedding guests still hanging about . . . . .49 minutes	

THE SECOND TIME

Attempting Insertion	Time Required
If groom ready to go . . . . .1 minute
If bride out the door . . . . .200 minutes

Honeymoon Etiquette:
HOW TO SPLIT THE WORK LOAD:

"You huff and I'll puff."

RAPTURE

U nfortunately, those who cherish in-bed communication will find, in most cases, actual talking (forming vowels with the lips and so on) nearly impossible. We therefore suggest the following signal system, invaluable for the exchange of vital information:

Number of Taps	Meaning
1	Not so hard.
2	Don't bite.
2½	You're an animal.
3	Let's switch.
4	Ooooooooooohhhhhhhh.
5	Let it ring.
5½	Not now dear.
6	Gently.
7	I'm levitating.
8	Slower.
9	Faster.
10	I can't see the TV.

STRANGE NOISES

The sounds of love—the groans and moans of arousal by a master technician—play a crucial role in communication between two lovers.

Sound	What It Means
Static	*"We need tuning."*
Wheezing	*"Slow down."*
Giggling	*"You missed."*
Short gasps	*"I'm close."*
Long gasps	*"I'm there."*
Squealing	*"I'm gone."*

Moaning:
    Pre-orgasmic
    Post-orgasmic
	
	"It's so good."
	"We're compatible."

Squishing	*"Need oil."*
Esperanto	*"Don't stop."*
Panting	*Partner tongue tied.*
Bells	*Wake-up call.*

SHOULD YOU MAKE LOVE UNDER THE COVERS?

S ome points to consider:

1. You won't be able to see your partner.

2. Weight of the blanket may inhibit movement (if it's a down-filled comforter, you may have to settle for a fetal position).

3. Under an especially heavy quilt, fresh air will be a problem—you may lose consciousness.

4. To the casual observer (Eyewitness News, for instance), the sight of a blanket bouncing up and down may prove alarming.

5. Friction may induce blanket sores.

Note: Making love under an electric blanket, turned up to "high," will increase your energy level.

UNDERCOVER SURVIVAL

Once asleep, men, especially large ones, present a problem: they're nearly impossible to move. Inevitably they will occupy 90 percent of the total mattress area, leaving the bride, especially if she's petite, barely enough room to yawn. Therefore, to reclaim your rightful share of the bed use:

1. Your elbow (four meaningful jabs should do it).

2. Your knee (aggressive, to be used only if he's actually hibernating).

3. Your maid of honor (many make house calls up to thirty days after the wedding ceremony).

4. Judo (a last-resort technique and favorite of Japanese brides who marry sumo wrestlers).

WHEN TO CHANGE POSITIONS

We recommend at least once every two hours—more often, however, should any of the following symptoms appear:*

One partner's head is scraping the floor

Appearance of mildew on either partner

One partner's shoulder is out the window

Leg cramp

Leg numb

Appearance of any bedsore larger than a postcard

One partner is comatose

Maid insists on changing the bedding

Only one partner's back is getting a suntan

Cobwebs

* Record: June 7, 1983. A couple in Bermuda won a champagne breakfast for two, plus a lifetime supply of liniment, after remaining in the missionary position for 17 hours, 22 minutes. They had to be separated in a laboratory.

HOW TO CHANGE POSITIONS

The typical sex manual lists nearly 40 positions but offers little advice concerning how to get into them. For newlyweds, this poses a problem: How to manage a smooth transition? How, for instance, to go from groom on top, bride on bottom, to bride on top, groom anywhere underneath, without disconnecting, or worse, rolling out into the hallway?

To facilitate this process:

1. Grasp partner firmly (use your rosin bag).

2. Be informative; explain what you intend to do.

3. Make sure you both agree.

4. Be certain there's room to maneuver.

5. Don't underestimate your partner's weight.

6. Don't overestimate your partner's height.

7. Don't give up if you become unattached—find each other and start over.

8. Never panic.

9. Remain cheerful if you feel something snap.

HOW LONG SHOULD IT TAKE TO CHANGE POSITIONS?*

From	To	Time Required
TRADITIONAL (Groom on top, bride on bottom)	NEO-TRADITIONAL (groom on bottom, bride at the threshold)	3 minutes, 14 seconds
CARIBBEAN CRUISE (Groom just floating, bride on brink)	POCONO RETREAT (Groom on bottom, bride demanding raise)	49 minutes, 2 seconds
NEWLYWED (*inexperienced*) (Groom on top, bride studying sex manual)	NEWLYWED (*anxious*) (Both on phone, consulting parents)	22 minutes
CONSERVATIVE MISSIONARY (Groom on top, bride wondering what he weighs)	LIBERAL MISSIONARY (Bride on top, bride wondering what she weighs)	10 seconds
SENSUOUS (Bride on top, groom on bottom)	CHASTE (Bride on top of mattress; groom underneath it)	35 minutes, ½ second

* If partner objects add 47 minutes.

SIGNS OF SEXUAL FATIGUE

(Disregard this page if you take steroids.)

Ignoring those danger signals that suggest, for the time being, you've had enough—gasping, dizziness, crossed eyes and spraying saliva—may cause severe physical damage and ruin the rest of your honeymoon. Consider, therefore, a recommended pause should you encounter any or all of the following:

Refrain from Sex For:	If Symptoms Include
One hour	Chirping Mussed hair Pulse rate in low 20's
Two hours	Moaning in Swedish Loss of muscle tone Repeated requests for chicken soup

Three hours	Inability to count
	   backwards from 2
	Difficulty recalling zip
	   code, area code,
	   genetic code

Four hours	Discomania

Five hours	Appearance of a third set of
	   teeth
	Persistent contraction of the
	   tongue muscle

Six hours	Change of blood type

HOW TO EAT IN BED

Should hunger beckon, those reluctant to leave their room will be happy to learn that, according to statistics, eating in bed is ten times safer than smoking in bed. We do suggest, however, observing the following precautions:

  1. Avoid "light" foods like popcorn and alfalfa. Not only do they offer little in the way of nourishment, but with the air conditioning set on "high" they will fly about the room and have to be swatted.

  2. Concentrate on "heavy" foods. They stay in your body longer (in the case of frank kabobs, 2 years and 3 months), thus providing sufficient energy for the wedding night, no matter how active. Suggestions:

Food	Will Sustain You For
Sushi	10 minutes
Gnocchi	10 days
Southern fried chicken:	
Georgia	3 days
Tennessee	5 days
New York	2 weeks
Chopped liver	1 week
Potato salad	1 day
Fried dumplings	2 days, 5 hours
Strudel:	
Light, flaky crust	24 hours
Normal crust	6 days
Big Mac	2 days
Little Mac	2 days

Pecan pie	4 days

Cheese cake:	
Italian	2 days
Jewish	2 weeks

Fried onion rings:	
Homemade	18 hours
Denny's	3 days

Fruitcake	Life

3. Avoid delicacies that shed. According to the AMA, crumbs are a leading cause of bedsores. Particularly notorious in this regard are potato chips, saltines and no-frills matzos.

4. Stay with "carefree" foods. Having to shuck oysters during arousal greatly reduces sexual enjoyment.

5. Remain alert. Abruptly dozing off in the middle of a bowl of chili and falling over sideways will ruin the most diligently Scotchgarded camisole.

6. Don't avail yourselves of items susceptible to spillage. Borscht and wonton soup are good examples.

7. Keep legs firmly crossed. Ignore this advice and the groom's eyes will bulge hideously should the entire top of a steaming pizza suddenly plunge into his lap.

8. Chinese food is permissible since MSG has been found to be effective in alleviating extreme cases of fetishism (failure to enjoy meaningful sex except with a block of tofu). Beware of fried rice, however, as it tends to get caught among the chest hairs and must be removed with tweezers.

9. Never moan with a knish in your mouth.

10. It is never permissible to wipe your hands on your partner.

RECREATIONAL POSITIONS

The great outdoors permits new opportunities for out-of-bed lovemaking, with choice of location limited only by your imagination and, in the case of skydiving, a fear of heights. Be aware, however, that these extra-curricular activities will consume far less energy than making love in the comfort of your bed (504 ergs per hour).

Location	Ergs Required
Horseback riding:	
Sidesaddle (at a trot)	.35
Bareback (at a gallop)	.68
On the golf course:	
The first hole (bride on top, groom teeing off) .	.19
The ninth hole (bride on bottom, groom	
putting)	.48
Miniature golf (both playing through)	.2
Scuba diving:	
Both wearing portable breathing devices (extra	
weight a factor)	.25
Both flipping out	.80
On a moped (a favorite in Bermuda and Jamaica) . . .	.17
To a calypso beat	.145
Skiing:	
On the slope	.22
On the lift (bride on top, groom rising)	.90

On a secluded beach:
    Tide out 7
    Tide in 274

In a pool:*
    Water temperature 75°F 96
    Water temperature 39°F 482

*Note: Bubbles may give you away.

CAUTION!
The Three Dangers of Outdoor Sex

1. Grass stains

2. Poison ivy

3. Splinters

HOW GOOD WAS IT?

The type of orgasm one has, be it clitoral, literal, penile or audible, is less important than the quality.

Good	Better	Best
Room moved	Earth moved	You moved
Fell out of bed	Did a cartwheel	Levitated
Butterflies	Waves of butterflies	Waves of butterflies in V-formation
Mirrors fogged	Wallpaper flocked	Can see breath
Unable to find pillow	Unable to find blanket	Unable to find partner
Can feel pulse	Heart pounding	Pacemaker overheating
Forgot phone number	Forgot zip code	Forgot name
Need a nap	Need deep sleep	Need a coma
Mustache loosened	Face lift came undone	Dental caps flew off
Firecrackers	Rockets	Applause

WAS IT GOOD FOR YOUR PARTNER?

S exologists assert that one facial expression is worth ten thousand moans. We therefore present the following scientific guide to your partner's pleasure.

| "Not bad" | "Lovely" | "You woke me up" |
| "Let's try that again" | "More" | "Dial 911" |

THING MOST OFTEN SAID AFTER SEX

"Was it good for you?"

THING MOST
OFTEN THOUGHT
AFTER SEX

"**M**ust floss."

MULTIPLE ORGASMS— HOW TO CELEBRATE

U until recently, even high achievers were entitled to only one orgasm. Now, thanks to human rights groups, it is permissible not only to enjoy many orgasms per sexual encounter, but also to keep count. For each climax, a thoughtful groom will reward his bride according to the following:

Orgasm	Appropriate Gift
1st	Paper or plastics
2nd	Cotton
3rd	Leather
4th	Linen, rayon, nylon, silk
5th	Wood
6th	Iron
7th	Copper, brass
8th	Electrical appliances or bronze
9th	Pottery or china
10th	Aluminum or tin
11th	Steel
12th	Linen, silk, nylon
13th	Lace
14th	Agate or ivory
15th	Crystal or glass
20th	China
25th	Silver
30th	Pearls
35th	Coral or jade
40th	Rubies or garnets
45th	Sapphires
50th	Gold
55th	Emeralds or turquoise
60th	Diamonds
75th	Diamonds or vitamins

HOW LONG SHOULD IT TAKE?

Take as long as you need—for the first climax, that is. For those who must budget their time, however, additional orgasms may cause a problem, especially if a conflict arises between the desire to continue lovemaking and an unreasonably early checkout time (midnight). You may therefore wish to take special notice of the chart below.

	Orgasm	Minutes Usually Required
FOR BRIDE	The first	. .6 to 11
	The second	.12 to 20
	If second only an echo	1
	The third	.21 to 40
	With mariachi band in the room	100
FOR GROOM	The first	18
	If he's been saving himself	1
	The second	.23
	Without erection	500
	The third	.62
	If he feels pressured	374

THE QUICKIE*

How fast can you lie down? Busy honeymooners have long pondered the problem of spontaneous sex, finding the time to make love when it's not particularly convenient—on a water slide, or during a game of pitch 'n' putt. Fortunately, with the aid of a reliable timing device and a reasonably flat surface, you and your partner will be able to go from arousal to golf in under one minute.

Activity	Seconds
Arousal	.5
Foreplay	.6
Fantasizing	.3
Discipline (optional)	.2
Insertion	½
Intercourse	.7
Climax	.4
Climax (with moans)	.6
Brushing each other off	.2
Checking for grass stains	.3
Resuming golf game	.1

*Does not apply on canoe trips down the Amazon.

DELAYING PLEASURE

T he bride who, during lovemaking, cries to her groom, "Don't stop now!" may be asking the impossible, especially if her partner has ventured beyond the point of no return.* Fortunately, for men not blessed with iron willpower, there is the mind-over-matter approach, a gentlemanly way to accommodate the bride without placing undue strain on the marriage.

To Delay Orgasm	Concentrate On
1 minute	Being stuck in traffic
2 minutes	Summer pet-care tips
3 minutes	Disposal of unwanted wedding gifts, such as the porcelain parakeet, the third blender....
4 minutes	Your new in-laws
5 minutes	How you'll enjoy their next visit
7 minutes	If they stay for two days
10 minutes	If they stay for two weeks
Indefinitely	If they move in

*The point at which a male is utterly unable to stop unless suddenly set upon by a playful beagle.

SIMULTANEOUS ORGASM

Considered by newlyweds to be the ultimate sharing experience, we offer two popular options:

Choice One *(traditional):*
Bride and groom climax together

Choice Two *(neighborly):*
Bride and groom climax at the same exact moment as the couple in the next room

Note: While choice one is, by far, the more sought after, choice two seems to occur more often at honeymoon resorts famous for either their group activities (Simon Says, pizza parties, etc.) or thin walls.

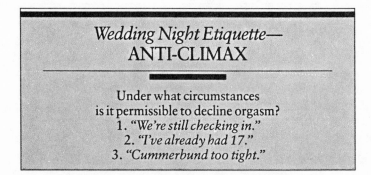

Wedding Night Etiquette—
ANTI-CLIMAX

Under what circumstances
is it permissible to decline orgasm?
1. *"We're still checking in."*
2. *"I've already had 17."*
3. *"Cummerbund too tight."*

THE NAP

C onsidered the perfect post-orgasmic remedy for newlyweds too exhausted to sleep, the nap serves to revive and refresh, enabling both partners to enjoy additional hours of lovemaking and then still have the strength not only to remain upright, but also to chew tough cuts of meat during intimate candlelight dinners. Suggested nap-duration times are as follows:

For Every	You Will Need A
20 minutes of lovemaking *(2 orgasms, 1 apiece)*	5-minute nap
40 minutes of lovemaking *(4 orgasms, 2 apiece)*	10-minute nap
60 minutes of lovemaking *(6 orgasms—bride 4, groom 2)*	15-minute nap
90 minutes of lovemaking *(7 orgasms—bride 3, groom 3, 1 unclaimed)*	25-minute nap
110 minutes of lovemaking *(no orgasm, but several interruptions by persistent magazine salesman)*	40-minute nap

BEYOND ORGASM

At this point, finding a dry spot may be difficult, especially if lovemaking has been dramatic. Over the next few nights, the problem will increase as both partners become less inhibited and begin to venture beyond the confines of the bed.

Night	Estimated Area of Moisture
The first	2" × 3"
The second	4" × 7"
The third	5" × 9"
The fourth	7" × 15"
The fifth	10" × 18"
The sixth	15" × 24"
The seventh	Complaints from couple across the hall.

DOING IT ON THE WET SPOT?

The debate goes on. A gallant groom will bear it, although he may not necessarily grin.

PATIENCE

How long does it take for the typical wet spot to dry? The information below is based on a room temperature of between 74 and 82 degrees Fahrenheit. *Note:* The natural drying process may be slightly hastened by fanning it.

If Wet Spot Is	Waiting Time
2" × 3"............................	17 minutes
5" × 9"............................	24 minutes
10" × 15".........................	51 minutes
17" × 24".........................	75 minutes
Fizzing...........................	148 minutes

CREATING A DRY SPOT

A bothersome task, but with a little ingenuity and cooperation, you needn't wait.

Five Ways to Eliminate the Wet Spot	Drying Time (in Minutes)
1. Blotting it	8
2. Fanning it	9
3. Blowing on it: Using mouth Using blow dryer	 7 4
4. Vigorously waving the sheet (quickest, but most exhausting)	2
5. Simply staring at it in awe	65

Additional Option	Minutes
Turning Mattress Over: Both partners help One partner still asleep	 2 5

ENDURANCE— HOW LONG CAN YOU LAST?

Newlyweds, especially those with sensitive skin, soon learn that intense lovemaking on a smooth, soft surface versus, say, a park bench, can mean the difference between two hours of bliss and two weeks of incapacitating bedsores. Consider, therefore, the following dermatological tips:

Type of Surface	Minutes Before Onset of Skin Irritation

SHEET MADE OF:

Satin	74

Silk	128

Flannel	61

Cotton: Sea Island	100
Canvas	3

Calico	39
Georgian period *(a little rougher)*	7

SOFA MADE OF:
Leather	19
Naugahyde	5

AND, FOR THE COURAGEOUS:

On hay *(real)*	13
(plastic)	1

HOW LONG CAN YOU STAY IN YOUR ROOM?

The ability to function without fresh air and sunshine varies according to each individual. In a room with a superior ventilation system, it may be possible to spend an entire two-week honeymoon in sexual bliss, sustained only by Meals on Wheels and a Visiting Nurse Service. Those unsure of their fortitude will know they've been inside too long should any of the following occur:

- New geologic era
- Postage rates go up
- Change of seasons
- Plants wilting
- New couple in your room

MOST COMMON HONEYMOON AFFLICTIONS

None of the following is cause for alarm. In most cases, the condition is remedied either by taking a brief intermission or turning up the air conditioning.

Fatigue

CAUSES:
1. Partner too heavy
2. Covers too heavy
3. Walking to the Poconos

Concussion

CAUSES:
1. Overly vigorous foreplay (partner fell on head)
2. Attempting laps across a heart-shaped tub

Painful Intercourse

CAUSES:
1. Magic Motion bed out of control
2. Groom standing too far away

Bedsores

CAUSES:
1. Too much honeymoon
2. Bargain sheets
3. Neglecting to change position

Anxiety

CAUSES:
1. Maid criticizing
2. Partner criticizing

Chafed Elbows

CAUSES:
1. Carpet burn
2. Mattress burn
3. Sand burn

Gagging

CAUSES:
1. Repulsive partner
2. Hair in throat (see Heimlich Maneuver)
3. Bride's first sight of groom in boxer shorts

Dislocated Back

CAUSES: 1. Attempting lotus position (groom on bottom, lotus on top)
2. Attempting to lower TV volume with toe

Bruises

CAUSES: 1. Fighting for your rightful share of the covers
2. Incautious outdoor location (edge of cliff; upon a dozing moose)

Shock

CAUSES: 1. First dose of morning mouth
2. Telling partner what gets you excited
3. Partner's reaction
4. Cold baby oil

Broken Fingernails

CAUSES: 1. Bride too passionate, groom's back too muscular
2. Impatience (attempting to pry frozen ice cream from container)

Chills

CAUSES: 1. Sunstroke
2. Lying in wet spot

Boredom

CAUSES: 1. Same partner
2. Following sex manual

Blackouts

CAUSES: 1. Stifling moans
2. Rapture
3. Discovering price of the room

Stomach Cramps

CAUSES: 1. Having sex too soon after eating
2. Tainted breath mints

Note: Three Most Uncommon Honeymoon Afflications:
1. Insomnia. 2. Abstention. 3. Morning sickness.

IN CASE OF EMERGENCY

Wedding Night CPR for the sexually overworked groom:

1. Lay groom on his back.

2. Open his mouth.

3. Tilt his head backward.

4. Ask him what's wrong.

5. Drop a meatball down his throat.

6. Wash it down with champagne.

NO LONGER ALONE

Once married, total privacy is a thing of the past. You therefore may wish to know how long you must be wed before you can abandon polite behavior and share the following intimacies:

Activity	Waiting Period
Gargle within hearing distance	1 month
Gargle noisily within hearing distance	2 months
Wear curlers to bed:	
Bride	3 weeks
Groom	3 months
Eat dinner in your underwear	5 months
Nag about money	7 months
Nag about sex	7 hours
Reveal major emotional disturbances (schizophrenia, belief in astrology)	6 months
Insist Mother come live with you	1 year
Insist she get out	5 years
Have sex:	
Once a day	2 months
Once a week	1 year
Once a month	3 years
Once a year	10 years
Ask personal questions	1 week
Answer personal questions	1 year

Part Six

HONEYMOON MEMORIES

FIRST NIGHT MEMORIES

(To Show Your Grandchildren)

Date of wedding night

Weight of bride ___ Weight of groom

Who was more nervous? □ Bride □ Groom

Who carried whom over the threshold?

Arousal initiated by: □ Bride □ Groom

How? □ Gentle blowing in ear □ Whining

□ Setting alarm □ Running bath water

□ Lowering TV volume

□ Other

How many times did we do it?

Who kept count? □ Bride □ Groom

□ People in adjoining room

We stopped counting after the ___ th time.

We passed out after the ___ th time.

Most sensuous position (missionary, etc.)

Most catastrophic position (back-to-back, etc.)

Locations

For the fun:	For the challenge:
☐ Bedroom	☐ Check-in desk
☐ Jacuzzi	☐ Pool
☐ Sofa	☐ Ocean
☐ Hot tub	☐ Airliner lavatory
☐ Shower	☐ Limo
☐ Floor	☐ Foxhole
☐ Other	☐ Other

Problems (personal):

☐ Bride locked herself in bathroom

☐ Groom locked himself in bathroom

☐ Bride locked groom in bathroom

☐ Groom couldn't find ice machine

☐ Groom fell into ice machine

Problems (general):

☐ No little mints on the pillow

☐ "Do Not Disturb" sign in Bulgarian

☐ Didn't know we had to bring our own towels

☐ Had to time-share the room

Most sensitive erogenous zone on:

Bride

Groom

Most appealing portion of anatomy on:

Bride:	*Groom:*
☐ *Eyes*	☐ *Deltoids*
☐ *Neck*	☐ *Triceps*
☐ *Chest*	☐ *Biceps*
☐ *Navel*	☐ *Quadriceps*
☐ *Behind*	☐ *Forceps*
☐ *Legs*	☐ *Chest*
☐ *Other*	☐ *Back*

Most ticklish erogenous zone on:

Bride

Groom

Most prevalent form of communication:

☐ *Panting*	☐ *Moaning*
☐ *Giggling*	☐ *Semaphore*
☐ *Gasping*	☐ *Squealing*

☐ *Clanging (enormous charm bracelet)*

Who was louder? ☐ *Bride*

☐ *Groom*

☐ *Crickets*

Who begged for mercy first? ☐ *Bride*

☐ *Groom*

☐ *Crickets*

Who fell asleep first? ☐ *Bride*

☐ *Groom*

☐ *Chaperon*

Most pleasant surprise for bride:

I thought he'd be _____

_____

I never thought he'd be so _____

_____

_____

Most pleasant surprise for groom:

I thought she'd be _____

_____

I never thought she'd be so _____

_____

THE
MORNING AFTER

He woke me up by

She woke me up by

Then we:

☐ *did it*

☐ *had breakfast*

☐ *both at same time*

Who got out of bed first?

☐ *Bride*

☐ *Groom*

GROUP PHOTO
(attach here)

LAST NIGHT MEMORIES

Date _____

Weight of bride _____

Weight of groom _____

Total number of times (permissible to approximate):

    For bride _____

    For groom _____

    For both _____

Most embarrassing moments:

    ☐ *Forgetting to remove "Just Married" sign*

    ☐ *Hotel service charge for 200 extra towels*

    ☐ *Discovering hidden microphone under bed*

    ☐ *Other*

_____

What we learned: _____

    Bride _____

    Groom _____

Our song _____